CORE Success and Life Coach Training

Accelerated Certification Training

This workbook belongs to:

_____

www.transformdestiny.com

CORE Success and Life Coach Training Manual

Printed in the United States of America

ISBN-13: 978-1-946607-07-2
ISBN: 1-946607-07-X

10 9 8 7 6 5 4 3 2 1

Welcome!

Welcome to our CORE Success and Life Coach Training. As you progress through this program, you will acquire a skill that will remain with you for the rest of your life. This class is based upon unique methods that have been developed and based upon proven techniques resulting from decades of research from the fields of successful coaching and Neuro-Linguistic Programming.

These classes are designed to be a hands-on learning experience. I encourage you to ask questions if you have them and please ask for my help if you need it. My goal is to provide a safe environment in which you are allowed to make mistakes and feel comfortable knowing that there is a trained professional nearby to assist you. With my help you will develop the skills you need.

After completing this course, you will be <u>qualified to be a professional Success and Life Coach</u> and may immediately begin practicing as such. However, additional education, culminating in becoming a Master Coach as well as TIME Techniques™ and Neuro-Linguistic Programming, is available for the student who is seriously interested in further knowledge, and enhanced professional status, in your chosen field.

Now please, sit back, relax, and enjoy the course!

Michael Stevenson

Michael Stevenson

President, Transform Destiny

About Your Instructor

Michael Stevenson MNLP, MTT, MHt is a professional certified Master Success and Business Coach, best-selling author and international speaker.

He has served more than 100,000 people around the world through his coaching programs, live events, radio show and online courses and is considered one of the world's foremost experts on the subjects of NLP and coaching. Michael is a dynamic presenter on a wide variety of topics ranging from personal growth to sales training.

As the owner of Transform Destiny Hypnosis, Michael maintains a rigorous schedule teaching people the importance of NLP and the role it plays in our results in all areas of life. His unique style is informative and entertaining, demonstrating Michael's instinctive ability to convey the most sophisticated topics to his audience in an easy to understand manner.

Between speaking engagements, Michael and his wife Kayla travel extensively, experiencing the wonders of the world and sharing the message that we are empowered.

Table of Contents

Notes

My Goals for this Workshop

1. _____
   _____
   _____
   _____

2. _____
   _____
   _____
   _____

3. _____
   _____
   _____
   _____

4. _____
   _____
   _____
   _____

5. _____
   _____
   _____
   _____

Notes

© 2018 Transform Destiny • www.transformdestiny.com • 800-497-6614

For Your Future Development

Future Trainings and Programs from Transform Destiny and Influence to Profit:

Business Track	**Certification Track**

The Inner Circle Coaching and Mastermind Program
Professional one-on-one coaching, mentoring, masterminds and business consulting

Business Track	Certification Track
Speaking to Profit 6 Days Speak and sell from stage with charisma and character, learn to sell from stage and learn the business of speaking	**NLP Master Trainer Development Program** TIME Master Trainer, Hypnotherapy Master Trainer Included, EFT Master Trainer Included, Coach Master Trainer Included Training Materials Included: PowerPoints, handouts, manuals, logistics manuals, etc.
Publishing to Profit 3 Days Write, Edit, Publish and Market your Book and use the Best-Seller Roadmap to success	**Trainer's Training & Evaluation** 18 Days – Master Practitioner Required TIME Trainer Included Hypnosis Trainer Included Coach Trainer and EFT Trainer Included
Marketing to Profit 4 Days Modern, proven marketing strategies to create more profit <u>and</u> freedom	**Master Practitioner Training** 15 Days -- Practitioner Prerequisite Master **TIME** Techniques Included Master Hypnotherapist Included Master Coach Included
Influence to Profit 3 Days Ethically influence and persuade people everywhere you go	**NLP Practitioner Training** 7 Days -- No Prerequisite TIME Techniques, Hypnotherapist, EFT and Coaching Included
Irresistible Elevator Pitch Formula™ 1 Day Learn to create new sales relationships and network like a pro	**Intro to NLP, FreeNLPHomeStudy.com or other home study courses** 16 - 20 Hour Courses, No Prerequisites

Notes

NLP Communication Model

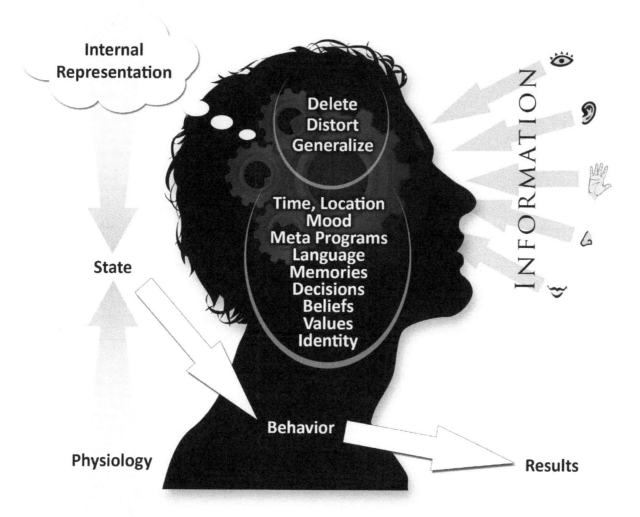

Remember: Perception is Projection

Notes

The Formula for Empowerment

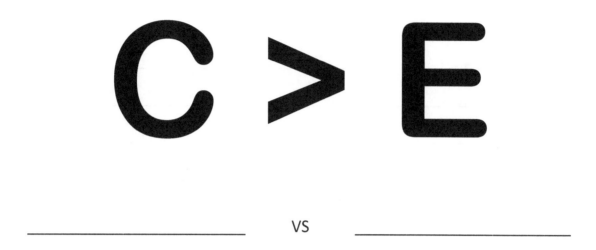

_____   VS   _____

Which side of the Cause and Effect formula are you on?   Are you the cause in your life, or are you at the effect side of things in your life?

Prediction: If there's something in your life that you're not happy with or that isn't going the way you want it to, you're living at the effect of someone something!

To truly be at cause, you must _____.

(Answers: results, reasons, take action.)

Notes

The Comfort Zone

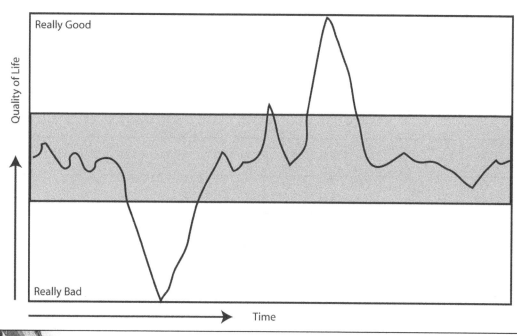

Notes

Principles for Success

1. Always Know Your _____.

_____

_____

_____

2. Take Real _____.

_____

_____

_____

3. Pay Attention to Your _____.

_____

_____

_____

4. Be Willing to Change Your _____.

_____

_____

_____

5. Always Focus on _____.

_____

_____

_____

6. Live Life with _____ and _____.

_____

_____

_____

(Answers: outcome, action, behavior, excellence, gratitude, integrity.)

Notes

States vs Goals

In NLP, we recognize a difference between states and outcomes. To set achievable goals or outcomes, you must know the difference:

Value or State	Goal or Outcome
Stated ambiguously	Stated specifically
Write affirmations	Write goals/outcomes
You can have it now	Time is involved
No steps – Just associate	Steps needed to get there
Infinite or not measurable	Measurable
Stated for self and/or others	Stated for self only

Notes

The Presuppositions of NLP

Convenient assumptions for creating profound shifts in your clients and yourself

1. Always **Respect** the other person's model of the world.

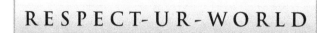

2. Behavior and change are to be evaluated in terms of context and **Ecology**.

3. Resistance in a client is a **Sign** of a lack of rapport. (There are no resistant clients, only inflexible communicators. Effective communicators accept and utilize all communication presented to them.)

4. **People** are not their behaviors.   (Accept the person; change the behavior.)

5. **Everyone** is doing the best they can with the resources they have available. (Behavior is adaptable, and the current behavior is the best choice available. Every behavior is motivated by a positive intent.)

6. **Calibrate** on behavior: The most important information about a person is that person's behavior.

7. The map is not the **Territory**. (The thoughts we have and the words we use are NOT the event or the item they represent.)

8. **(U) You** are in charge of your mind, and therefore your results.

9. People have all the **Resources** they need to succeed and to achieve their desired outcomes. (There are no unresourceful people, only unresourceful states.)

10. All procedures should increase **Wholeness**.

11. There is **Only** feedback! (There is no failure, only feedback.)

12. The meaning of communication is the **Response** you get.

13. The **Law** of Requisite Variety: (The system/person with the most behavioral flexibility controls the system.)

14. All procedures should be **Designed** to increase choice.

Notes

Prime Directives of the Subconscious

1. **Preserves the body**

2. **Runs the body**
   Has a blueprint of body as it is now, and of the body in perfect health

3. **Stores memories**
   Temporal (in relationship to time) and atemporal (not in relationship to time)

4. **Is the domain of the emotions**

5. **Organizes <u>all</u> memories**
   Uses a Gestalt on the timeline

6. **Represses memories with unresolved negative emotions**

7. **Presents repressed memories for resolution**
   To release emotions

8. **Is symbolic**
   Uses and responds to symbols

9. **Takes everything personally**
   The basis of Perception is Projection

10. **Works on the principle of least effort**
    Takes the path of least resistance

11. **Does not process negatives**
    Don't think of a blue tree

12. **May keep the repressed emotions repressed for protection**

13. **Is a highly moral part of you**
    The morality you were taught and accepted

14. **Enjoys serving, needs clear orders to follow**

15. **Controls and maintains all perceptions**
    Both regular and telepathic, and transmits them to the conscious mind

16. **Generates, stores, distributes and transmits all "energy"**

17. **Maintains instincts and generates habits**

18. **Needs repetition until a habit is installed (the quicker, the better)**

19. **Is programmed to continually seek more and more**
    There is always more to discover

20. **Functions best as a whole integrated unit**
    Does not need parts to function

Notes

© 2018 Transform Destiny • www.transformdestiny.com • 800-497-6614

How the Mind Interprets

Loveisnowhere

Theytoldhimtobeatthefrontdoor

They are visiting relatives

Would you rather have an elephant eat you or a gorilla?

How many times does the letter "F" appear in the sentence in the box?

(include both upper and lower case)

> **Finished files are the result of years of scientific study combined with the experience of many years of experts.**

Paris

in the

the Spring

The sentence below is printed backward. Read through the sentence once from right to left.

".rat eht saw tac ehT"

Notes

What is Coaching?

Coaching is a relationship where the coach helps the client achieve their goals, visions and dreams. The job of a success coach is to help the client help themselves.

Any kind of coaching requires a longer-term relationship with clients. You will help them define goals, eliminate negative emotions, eliminate limiting decisions, collapse negative anchors, and motivate them (and teach them to motivate themselves) and hold them accountable.

Coaching Is Not...	Coaching Is...
Content	Structure
Being Their Friend	Outcome Oriented and Solution Focused
Giving Advice	Based on Clear, Direct Feedback
Parenting	Accountability
Being Superior	Being Supportive
Short-Term Fix	Long-Lasting Results
Creating Dependence	Creating Independence by Leveraging Personal Resources

"Whether you think you can, or you think you can't, you're right." - Henry Ford

"Your clients will be your clients because they are out of rapport with their unconscious minds." - Milton Erickson

Notes

Areas of Life for Coaching

Notes

The Three 'C's of Success Coaching

1. <u>C</u>ommitment to Success

Both you and your client must be 100% committed to success. Coaching for mediocrity will get mediocre results. Your and your client's goals should always be for total success.

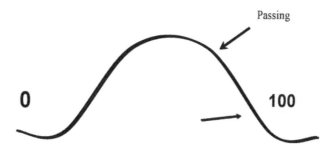

2. <u>C</u>ommitment to Action

You and your client should always end with a "contract" stating what the client will do between now and their next session. Years of social psychology research have shown that when a person makes a specific verbal and written commitment to action, they will do everything in their power to remain consistent with that commitment. Having your client sign their Action Contract will help insure their success. An example Action Contract is available on page 105.

3. <u>C</u>reating Accountability from Session to Session

Your job is to hold your client accountable. When your client commits to something and then doesn't follow through, you must let the client know that's not acceptable and won't help them find success. Determine what the obstacles were and come up with ways around them.

Notes

Requisites for Success – PAW

For success to happen with your client, they need to realize three things:

- **Possibility:** Your client has to believe the goals are possible.

- **Ability:** They need to know they are capable of achieving them.

- **Worthiness:** They need to believe they deserve to achieve them.

Notes

CORE Method Overview

1. Connecting with Your Client

2. Collecting Info, Giving Feedback

3. Asking Powerful Questions

4. Setting Outcomes

5. Creating an Action Plan

6. Getting Commitment

7. Creating Momentum

Notes

Step 1 – Connecting with Your Client

Rapport is a state of feeling *as if* you like someone. People like people who are like themselves.

All coaching must be done from a place of rapport. Without rapport, the connection needed for effective coaching is difficult to attain, at will. The client must always trust the coach.

Communication

Communication can be both verbal and non-verbal. At any given time, we're communicating more than we're saying. The reason is, our non-verbal communication is far more meaningful than the words we speak.

Communication is made of the following components:

Words	**7%**
Tonality	**38%**
Physiology	**55%**

Vocal tone and physiology are important in communicating congruence and suggestions.

This is important in establishing rapport, as explained on the next page.

Notes

Gaining Rapport

When people are like each other, they tend to like each other. The NLP process of rapport creates a feeling *as if* the participants like each other. Rapport is a process of responsiveness, and not necessarily "liking."

Rapport is established by pacing and leading. The Following are major elements of rapport:

Physiology (55%)

Posture

Gestures

Facial expressions and blinking

Breathing

Tonality (38%)

Voice

Tone	(pitch)
Tempo	(speed)
Timbre	(quality)
Volume	(loudness)

Four Indicators of Rapport
1.
2.
3.
4.

Words (7%)

Predicates

Key words

Common experiences and associations

Content chunks

You can also match one part of the body with another (for example, breathing with finger tapping). This is called cross-mirroring, and can highly covert.

Notes

Step 2 – Collecting Info, Giving Feedback

When meeting with the client, it's important that you find out exactly where the client is. You'll ask questions to find out where the client is now (since the last session, or in general, if it's the first session). An example of an Action Plan Worksheet that can be used in this step is available on page 105.

If this is a follow-up session, you'll want to compare your client's recent progress with the commitments they made in the previous session. You will hold the client accountable and find out what roadblocks and obstacles prevented them from attaining their goals. This feedback will feed forward into the goals you help your client to create to do by the next session.

If you are working with a new client, this interview process will be used to determine where they are now and what they have done in the past to achieve their outcomes.

Give constructive feedback on progress using the Feedback Sandwich. Identify areas that need attention and improvement based on progress.

Powerful Questions for Feedback/Interviewing

- Why are you here? (Why else? Why else?)

- Where are you now?

- What steps have you taken?

- What are your results?

- What do you need to do differently to get your outcome?

- What do you need to have learned now in order to get your outcome?

Notes

© 2018 Transform Destiny • www.transformdestiny.com • 800-497-6614

Important Concepts for Feedback

There is no Failure

One of the most crucial concepts in self-development is the presupposition that there is no failure – only feedback.

This is an example of an NLP *reframe*. While the circumstances remain unchanged, this presupposition changes the focus of your client from being problem-orientated to solution-oriented.

The fact is, most successful people do not see life in terms of failures and successes, but rather in terms of successes and feedback. Anything that is not success is evaluated for what can be learned and those learnings are incorporated into the next attempt.

> *"I have not failed 700 times. I have not failed once. I have succeeded in proving that those 700 ways will not work. When I have eliminated the ways that will not work, I will find the way that will work."*
>
> *"Many of life's failures are experienced by people who did not realize how close they were to success when they gave up."*
>
> *Thomas Edison*

> *"I never lose. I either win or I learn."*
>
> *Unknown*

Notes

The Feedback Sandwich

After years of research on feedback in the field of NLP, we've found that there is an effective way to give and receive it. The result is what's known as the Feedback Sandwich, and it's formulated in such a way that the conscious and unconscious minds can both accept feedback without bruising the ego.

1. **One Great Thing**

   Tell them one thing they did very well. For instance, "You did a fantastic job handling that problem you were talking about last week. That was very resourceful."

2. **The Stretch**

   Tell them one or two things they can improve. For example, "And I think next time, you should focus more on the result, rather than the problem. Remember, you get what you focus on, so focus on what you want." It's important not to overload them with details they can't handle. Only give them feedback on things that will "move the needle."

3. **Positive Overall Comment**

   Tell them, overall, how they did well. For example, "And overall, you are making excellent progress toward your goals. You've really come far!"

For the client to get the most benefit from feedback, it's important that they

a) Listen quietly to the feedback.

b) Do not justify or explain. When we justify our actions, we do not absorb the feedback. At the end of the process, your client should be instructed to simply say, "Thank you," and fully consider the feedback.

Notes

© 2018 Transform Destiny • www.transformdestiny.com • 800-497-6614

The Power of Self-Forgiveness

One of the biggest obstacles to progress is often holding a self-grudge when something doesn't go right.

People tend to put so much effort into, "kicking themselves," that it freezes them and drains their energy for moving forward.

We have to recognize when this happens and reverse it as soon as possible.

I often have my clients stop what they're saying (this is a pattern interrupt), and I say, "Repeat after me: I (name) FORGIVE MYSELF!"

I have them repeat it until I can hear the shift in their voice and their energy and make them commit to me that what happened is now in the past, and dwelling on it is doing them no good.

Notes

Step 3 – Asking Powerful Questions

Asking empowering questions is a skill that most people lack, but that can be easily learned. Asking powerful questions is one of the most important coaching skills.

This consists of dialoguing with the client about the area of life being coached for. Your job is to dig up limiting decisions, limiting beliefs, negative emotions, and any other obstacle in your client's way, and to coach them through those obstacles.

Questions are the primary way to explore your client's issues and help them to overcome the hurdles.

Powerful questions usually have the following characteristics:

1. **What-Based Questions**
   Asking "why" questions rarely produces powerful results. Why focuses on motivation, which can be important, but "what" questions focus on solutions.

   "What's important to you about that?"
   "What do you want?"
   "What could prevent you from achieving your goals?"

2. **Action-Oriented**
   Thinking about results isn't enough. Your client must take action to achieve their outcomes. Your questions should always lead the client toward action.

   "What will you do by next week to insure that happens?"
   "What will your next step be when you leave the office today?"
   "What other options do you have?"
   "What are you unwilling to change?"
   "What can you learn from this?"
   "What will you do differently next time?"
   "What can you do that will make a difference now?"

Notes

3. **Orientation to Goals**

   Powerful questions should always be goal-oriented, rather than problem oriented. Focus on Solutions and Goals, rather than picking apart problems and obstacles.

4. **Oriented to the Future**

   Coaching should always focus on what the client can do now, and in the future. Never on the past, with the exception of past positive resources that can be used in the future.

5. **Powerful Presuppositions**

   These questions take the following structure:

   What + you + verb + future positive?

   "What will you change next week for success?"
   "What resource can you leverage to meet your monthly sales goal?"

Notes

Questions that Challenge Obstacles

When listening to your client, words can never be as rich as their own internal meaning and symbols in their mind. Even their symbols are based on filters that are out of their conscious awareness, and so, are not accurate representations of "reality."

These impoverished views are often viewed by the client as obstacles. But, often times, they are only <u>perceived</u> obstacles. Challenging these statements will allow you to shift their awareness and put your clients in touch with more resources.

Uncontested Opinions

Everybody has opinions, but often opinions can be quite limiting, especially when the opinion is stated as fact. Opinions are subjective, by nature, and based on beliefs – not facts. A client may give you their opinion, or even the opinion of others, as if it were fact. By pointing these opinions out, you allow the client to evaluate the opinion consciously.

Another form of opinion is the comparison. When you hear your client using words like easier, harder, good, bad, better, worse, etc., your client is giving a subjective opinion that they likely view as fact.

Finally, adverbs, like definitely, obviously, truly, clearly, plainly, are uncontested opinions. Perhaps it is obvious to them, but not to others.

All of these kinds of statements can be challenged and explored using the following types of response:

- "According to whom/what?"

- "Who says?"

- "Better/worse/easier/harder than what?"

- "Bad/good compared to what?"

- "Obvious/true/clear/plain according to who?"

Generalizations

Generalizations can be a good thing. Our minds have too much to think about already, so they can save our brains processing time. However, generalizations can also prevent us from

Notes

learning new things. When we generalize from a thing or two that aren't representative of the whole, we make bad generalizations. We leave out some of the 2.3 million bits that might hold contrary information.

Common generalizations contain universal words, such as all, every, always, never, everything, and nothing. When you client gives you generalizations, challenge them in the following ways:

- "Has there ever been a time when you did (or didn't)?"

- "Never?"

- Or provide a counter-example, "Donald Trump certainly doesn't have that problem."

Pressure Words

Pressure words are those words of necessity that we put upon ourselves. Words like must, mustn't, should, shouldn't, ought to, ought not.

Usually, these words are based on rules the person has in their life, the validity of which they may never have challenged.

You can challenge these words using the following types of responses:

- "What would happen if you did/didn't?"

- "Who says you should/shouldn't?"

- "Just suppose you could. What would that be like?"

Notes

Frozen Verbs

Also called Nominalizations, frozen verbs are processes which have been frozen in time and turned into a noun (a thing). Words such as communication, decision, failures and stress are frozen verbs.

The test to find out if a noun is a frozen verb is to ask yourself the following question:

"Can I put [noun] into a wheelbarrow?"

If the answer is no, as is the case with words like failures and stress, then the word is actually a frozen verb, not a noun.

The problem with frozen verbs is that they are "stuck." A decision is a thing, and therefore, cannot be changed. But when you turn the frozen word "decision," back into "decide," it becomes a verb again, which opens more options.

Client: I've already made the <u>decision</u>. I can't leave my day job to pursue a silly dream of being rich.

Coach: What if you could <u>decide</u> something different. What would that be like?

Or

Client: I don't know what to do, I've got all this <u>stress</u>.

Coach: What is it that is <u>stressing</u> you that you could handle differently?

When you hear a frozen verb, simply turn it back into a noun and you offer the client more choices for success.

Examples of Frozen Verbs Heard in Coaching

Results	Profit	Loss
Stress	Decision	Frustration
Trust	Feelings	Actions
Commitment	Communication	Accountability

Notes

Questions for Clarity

Pattern	Response
DISTORTIONS	
1. Mind Reading: Claiming to know someone's internal state. Ex: "She thinks I'm stupid."	"How do you know she thinks you're stupid?"
2. Value Judgements: Value judgments where the person doing the judging is left out. Ex. "It's not good to be greedy."	"Who says it's not good?" "According to whom?" "How do you know it's not good?"
3. Cause and Effect: Where cause is wrongly put outside the self. Ex: "She makes me want to cry."	"How does what she's doing cause you to <u>choose</u> to cry?" (Also, Counter Example, or "How Specifically?")
4. False Equality: Where two experiences are interpreted as being synonymous. Ex: "Buying me flowers is manipulative."	"How does him buying flowers mean he's manipulating?" "Have you ever bought flowers for someone you liked?"
5. Presuppositions: Ex: "If my wife knew how angry I get, she wouldn't do that." There are three Presuppositions in this sentence: (1) I get angry, (2) My wife acts in some way, and (3) My wife doesn't know I suffer.	(1) "How do you choose to get angry?" (2) "How is she (re)acting? (3) "How do you know she doesn't know?"
GENERALIZATIONS	
6. Universal Generalizations: Universal Generalizations such as all, every, never, everyone, no one, etc. Ex: "He never lets me get a word in!"	Find Counter Examples. "Never?" "What would happen if he did?"
7. Necessity Words: As in should, shouldn't, must, must not, have to, need to it is necessary. Ex: "I have to let her have her way." **8. Possibility/Impossibility Words:** As in can/can't, will/won't, may/may not, possible/impossible. Ex: "I couldn't possibly tell him the truth."	a. "What would happen if you did?" ("What would happen if you didn't?" Also, "Or?" b. "What prevents you?" ("What would happen if you did?")
DELETIONS	
9. Frozen Verbs: Process words which have been frozen in time, making them nouns. Ex: "There is no communication here."	"Who's not communicating what to whom?" "How would you like to communicate?"
10. Vague Verbs: Ex: "She shamed me."	"How, specifically?"
11. Simple Deletions: Ex: "I am uncomfortable." **12. Unspecified Person/Thing:** Fails to specify a person or thing. Ex: "They don't want me to be happy." **13. One-Sided Comparisons:** As in good, better, best, worst, more, less, most, least. Ex: "She's a better person."	a. "About what/whom?" b. "Who, specifically, doesn't want you to be happy?" c. "Better than whom?" "Better at what?" "Compared to whom, what?

Notes

Step 4 – Setting Outcomes

A coaches job is to help your client decide on their outcomes and to break them down into an actionable step-by-step plan that is SO easy, they couldn't not do it.

It's simple enough to ask the following question:

"What is it you'd like to achieve in (area of coaching)? What else? What else?"

_____

_____

_____

_____

Often, our clients can't see their own full potential, so sometimes we have to nudge them. Don't be afraid to challenge them to make their goals a little bigger.

Notes

© 2018 Transform Destiny • www.transformdestiny.com • 800-497-6614

Creating Achievable Outcomes (NLP)

1. **Get the specific outcome**
   a. What will you see, hear and feel when you have it?
   b. Make it compelling

2. **Find out their present situation**
   a. "Where are you now in relation to your outcome?"

3. **Get their evidence procedure**
   a. "How will you know when you have it?"

4. **Is it congruently desirable?**
   a. "What will this outcome get for you or allow you to do?" "Are you sure you want it?"

5. **Is it self-initiated and self-maintained?**
   a. "Is it only for you?"   "Are you the only person in charge of your results?"

6. **Is it appropriate in all contexts?**
   a. "Where, when, how and with whom do you want it?" "Are there drawbacks in any of these contexts?"

7. **Check for ecology**
   a. "For what purpose do you want it?" "What will you lose or gain if you get it?"

8. **Future pace it with a specific date**
   a. "It is now January 12, 2025 and…" (Dissociated)

9. **Write it present tense**
   a. "I have…" "I am…" or "I do…"

10. **Get the outcome with positive language**
    a. "What specifically do you want?" (Not what you don't want)

11. **Establish and write resources**
    a. "What personal resources do you have that will allow you to achieve this?"
    b. "Do you know anyone else who has achieved it? What resources did they have?"
    c. "Imagine you have it now. Other than those mentioned, what resources did you use to get it?"

What will happen if you get it?   What will happen if you don't get it?

What won't happen if you get it?   What won't happen if you don't get it?

Notes

SMART Goals

Traditional goal-setting has used the SMART acronym for setting goals. This version of the SMART acronym has been modified to include the newer, more powerful ways of setting achievable outcomes, discovered in the field of NLP.

To be the most successful, make sure your goals are:

S	**Simple** **Specific** **See Yourself**
M	**Measurable** **Meaningful to You**
A	**As If Now** **Achievable** **All Areas of Your Life**
R	**Realistic** **Responsible / Ecological**
T	**Timed** **Toward What You Want**

Notes

How to Set Outcomes

Everybody knows that you should set long-term and short-term goals, but most people go about it the wrong way, setting long term goals first, then trying to figure out the first step, second step, third step, and so forth.

One of the most important contributions of NLP and TIME Techniques to the area of goal setting is the concept of working **backward** from your long-term goals.

When you have a long-term goal in mind – for instance, setting a one year gold of, "I now make $1M" – it's incredibly difficult to determine the first step. What is the first step to making a million dollars in a year? If you knew, you'd probably have it now!

However, if you start with the long term goal and work your way backwards, you'll have a much better chance of devising an achievable outcome.

Starting at the one year gold of a million dollars, where would you have to be nine months from now to achieve it? You certainly wouldn't be at step one! You'd be "almost there." You'd obviously have to be making an income conducive to a million dollar year. So, your nine month goal may be, "I now sell my own products, bringing in $200,000 each month in active (sales) and passive (investments) income."

Knowing that, where would you have to be in six months to achieve that nine month goal? "I now have my own corporation and my first product or service is developed and ready to sell. My passive income is bringing me $2,500 per month."

Where would you have to be in three months? Perhaps, "I have now done all the research about how to incorporate a business. I am investigating and researching products and/or services in my area of expertise that I can develop and/or improve upon. I have researched day trading and investing to create a passive income and I'm ready to start purchasing investments."

Where would you have to be in one month? "I have left my 'day job' to pursue my goal of making $1M in the next eleven months. I have leveraged my savings and have enough money to survive and invest for six months."

Where would you need to be in a week? "I have given my employer four weeks notice. I am investigating how to best leverage my savings, escrow and possibly my retirement fund to achieve this goal."

All outcomes become more achievable when you work backwards.

Notes

Step 5 – Create an Action Plan

The action plan consists of short-term action items that the client will be working on between now and the next session to move closer to their outcomes. These action items should be smaller steps toward the larger goals.

Often you clients will ask you, "What should I do?" It's important, as a coach, that you avoid offering outright advice to your clients. Rather, you should help them to discover what is right for themselves. For example:

Coach: "What will you do between now and next week to increase your sales?"

Client: "What should I do?"

Coach: "What is it you think you should do? What steps can you take that will get results?"

Powerful Action Plan Questions

- "What will you do between now and next session?"

- "How will you finish the task at hand?"

- "What is the last step you need to achieve that? Let's work backwards."

- "How has your outcome changed since our previous session?"

- "What must you do differently this time, in order to achieve your desired results?"

- "What don't you want to do that you know you must?"

Use the Action Plan sheet on page 39 to formulate the Action Steps your client will take by the next session.

Notes

Step 6 – Get Commitment

In order for your coaching relationship to be powerful, your client has to learn to make commitments, and then to be accountable for them. The following techniques work very well for gaining commitment.

Be Specific

Be specific in creating the Action Plan. If your clients Action Steps are too nebulous or vague, they will have too much "wiggle room" and may not take the step. Create specific steps for them to take.

Create a Time Limit

Create a time limit for the Action Step. If your client is presented with a deadline, they are much more likely to take action than if they had an indefinite amount of time to complete the Action Step.

Get Verbal and Written Agreements

The field of social psychology has done many studies in the area of commitment. One common thread is that a person will go to extraordinary ends to be consistent with the verbal and written commitments they have made. This is ingrained deep within our societal values and rules and is not easily overcome.

When your client makes their action plan, get their verbal and written commitment that they will do everything in their power to take action, complete their Action Steps and succeed at each one. During the next session, review their Action Steps and hold them accountable. Find out what feedback they received and help them incorporate that feedback into their next Action Plan.

If you are working with your client over the phone, simply fax them the Action Plan and have them sign it and fax it back.

Notes

© 2018 Transform Destiny • www.transformdestiny.com • 800-497-6614

Step 7 – Creating Momentum

One thing is certain, without motivation and momentum, achieving even the most rudimentary outcomes is difficult. As a coach, you want to help your client create both motivation and momentum.

Most people don't know how to create either, but we are going to share some very powerful techniques from the field of NLP with you.

Submodalities

Most people don't realize it, but our minds are just like computers. And just as computers have a basic computer language that consists of ones and zeros, our minds have a basic language made up of:

- Pictures

- Sounds

- Feelings

- Smells

- Tastes

- Self-Talk

It may not be immediately obvious, but just like changing the ones and zeros of a computer file change the way the computer reads and interprets the file, changing the qualities of our thoughts in our minds will also change the way we interpret them.

The way we change our thoughts is not by changing the pictures, sounds and feelings, but by changing the qualities of those modalities. These qualities are called *submodalities*.

These submodalities consist of the elements on the following page…

Notes

Visual

- Color or Black and White

- Brightness

- Size

- Distance

- Location

- Associated or Dissociated

- Framed or Panoramic

- Movie or Still

- Focus

Auditory

- Location

- Direction

- Internal/External

- Volume

Kinesthetic

- Location

- Size

- Shape

- Intensity

Notes

By changing those qualities, you can alter the way a person feels about nearly any situation or subject. Try this:

Think of a time that you felt motivated. When you think of that time, do you have a remembered image of it in your mind? Good, just temporarily, take that picture in your mind's eye and push it away from you – all the way out to the corner of the room, make it small and dark, the size of a postage stamp, and see your body in the picture.   Now, how do you feel about it now? For most people, the motivation will have disappeared.

Let's not leave it like that, so as quickly as you can, have that picture come racing at you at about 100 miles per hour, it sounds like a racecar and a jet, it explodes big and bright in your face, the picture wraps around you and you jump into your body so you're inside the picture. It seems very much more motivating, doesn't it? For most people, it will.

Now, this was all just for fun. So now you can allow that picture to go right back to where it was before we started playing with it. Just allow it to go right back where it was.

This is a very powerful technique. Any time someone has a goal they would like to achieve, ask them to think of it, and notice the picture they make in their mind's eye. Once they have that, begin by having them adjust their submodalities.

Start with color or black and white. Have them increase the colors and make them more vivid. If that makes them want it more, great! If not, maybe they need more muted colors. Have them turn it down. Next, work with brightness. Turn it up. If that works for them, leave it, otherwise, try turning it down. Have them adjust all the submodalities to just the right intensity that they *really* want this goal and it will create amazing amounts of motivation and momentum.

Notes

Tonality of Authority

Voice Tonality   **Notes:**

W ⟹ W↗   **W.** = Question   _____

_____

W ⟹ W⟹   **W.** = Statement   _____

_____

W ⟹ W↘   **W.** = Command   _____

When dealing with your clients, use a command tonality to communicate congruence and confidence.

Notes

© 2018 Transform Destiny • www.transformdestiny.com • 800-497-6614

Anchoring

Anchoring happens when the brain links two things together neurologically. We are always using anchors, all the time. When you see a movie or a picture from the past that moves you, hear a song that takes you back, feel a feeling that reminds you of another place and time, or smell that smell of home cooking, those are all anchors. They are all linked to past experiences and bring back the emotions, immediately.

We can use this process to our advantage. While anchoring is a subject that is far to in-depth for this weekend training, we can begin to learn about anchors and use some of the simpler techniques.

There are Four Basic Steps to Anchoring

1. **Recall** a past, vivid experience.
2. **Anchor** at the peak.
3. **Change** the person's state.
4. **Evoke the State** using the anchor.

The Six Keys to Creating Successful Anchors:

1. The **Timing** of the anchor.

2. The **Uniqueness** of the stimulus.

3. The **Replication** of the stimulus.

4. The **Number** of times applied.

5. The **Intensity** of the state.

6. The **Physiology**/Breathing accompanying the state at the time of anchoring.

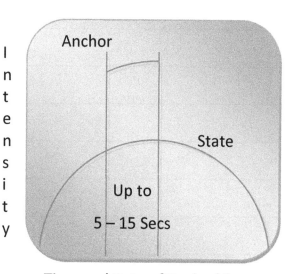

Time and Rate of Peak of State

An anchor should be held for a minimum of 5 – 15 seconds.

Notes

To create an anchor, you'll want to get your client into an intense state. Naturally occurring states that are happening in the moment are the most powerful. Next most powerful are remembered states. And finally, if the client can't have the state or remember having it, they can act as if they were in that state. This is the weaker of the three options, but sometimes is the only option.

To get the client into a remembered state, ask the following: "Can you remember a time when you felt totally (name emotion, for instance, motivated)? Good, can you remember a specific time? Good, as you go back to that time now, in your mind's eye, float down into your body, looking through your own eyes, see what you saw, hear what you heard and really feel that feeling of (name emotion – i.e., motivation)."

When the client begins to go into state, touch them in a way that is unique and repeatable at the peak of their state for 5 – 15 seconds.

Once the anchor is set, all the client has to do is touch that same spot at the same location with the same pressure and intensity and they will immediately return to that emotional state.

Stacking Anchors

It's useful to "stack" anchors, creating very powerful states at the touch of a finger. In NLP, we call this a Resource State. In this case, simply have the client get into a peak state, and anchor it in one spot – say the third knuckle of their index finger on their right hand. Then, have then get into another state and *anchor it in the same spot*. This will create a powerful anchor that will trigger both states.

You can stack the same state multiple times in order to make the anchor stronger, or you can anchor multiple states on the same anchor, in order to make it more powerful.

Teach this technique to your clients, as it will help them to create amazingly powerful resource states that will help them achieve their outcomes.

Future Pacing Pain and Pleasure

Many studies have shown the effectiveness of Future Pacing. It has been proven that the unconscious mind does not know the difference between something that happens in reality, and something that is imagined intensely, with full detail.

Because of this, you can use suggestive language to take your client's unconscious mind to a time in the future when they have achieved their goal. If they imagine it full enough, it will become more and more of a reality for them. This associates great pleasure to achieving that outcome.

Notes

There are times when a little pain is useful. Taking your client out into the future and showing them the future pain of inaction can be a great initial motivator.

Numerous studies have shown that when a client is shown a painful future, then shown a pleasurable future in follow-up, they are much more likely to take action than if they had only been shown the pleasurable choice.

Once you know your client, you'll be able to predict those things that might be painful for them to not change, and can use that to help motivate them to their ultimate goals.

Notes

CORE Method Overview

1. **Connecting with Your Client**

2. **Collecting Info, Giving Feedback**

3. **Asking Powerful Questions**

4. **Setting Outcomes**

5. **Creating an Action Plan**

6. **Getting Commitment**

7. **Creating Momentum**

Notes

Identifying Emotional Benefits

Sometimes, a client has a negative pattern that they need to break, but they are receiving a benefit from the pattern – even if unconsciously – that is providing more value than letting go of the problem does. This is called **Secondary Gain**. In situations like these, it's important to get at the underlying emotional need and help the client find a more appropriate way to meet that need. This is an example script for doing just that.

"So, John, in our last session, you said you weren't going to take any more time off of work. You said you were going to focus on your outcome and double your income. Yet you took two days off. So, when you took those days off after our session, I'm guessing that you came to some sort of an emotional crossroad, a point of decision if you will. Is that correct? I mean, you didn't just accidentally forget to go to work two days, did you? You did decide, did you not?

"Okay, so when you came to that crossroad, I'm guessing that you probably weighed your options. You knew you were going to have to talk to me about it, but the temptation to take some time off was so compelling it overshadowed the negative consequences, correct? So I'm curious, what was it that pushed you over the edge, and allowed you to do that? What was it that you thought the days off would give you, regardless of whether or not they actually did? What was the emotion you were going for?"

Now at this point, your client will probably say "I don't know." This is the *make-it-or-break-it* part of the interview. Whatever you do, DO NOT SAY ANYTHING EXCEPT "I know you don't know, but if you did know, what would you say?" Sit back, be quiet, and let them talk it out. DO NOT OFFER SUGGESTIONS UNDER ANY CIRCUMSTANCES!!! It is important to realize that offering help to your client at this point will destroy the interview completely and literally ruin the effectiveness of the second session – even if you offer the smallest bit of advice.

Here's what will happen. Usually, they struggle, say they don't know a couple of times, and then start telling you a story about what happened. Pay no attention to the story. It will only distract you. Turn your ear toward one thing and one thing only – an emotional word. Once you have that, you have the key. Here's an example of a typical response...

"I don't know, I just got so buried in work. There I was Thursday morning, and I was going crazy because I didn't know what to do work on first that day, on top of that I was stressed out because my boss barked at me and threatened to fire me if I didn't hit my quota. Plus I had an appointment with my real estate agent to talk about the new house. So, there I was, nervous, stressed out, and wanting some time to get away, because in the past, taking time

Notes

© 2018 Transform Destiny • www.transformdestiny.com • 800-497-6614

off from work made me feel confident that I could handle the situations of the day more effectively, so playing hooky would seem to take away all that stress, I guess."

Now at the surface, we might think that the client wanted to relax, but that word never came up. The only word that came up which was a positive emotional benefit was the word "confident".

If you use any other word other than confident, you are putting words into their mouth, reading their minds (inaccurately), and not focusing on the real issue at hand. IF YOU USE ANY WORD OTHER THAN THE WORD THEY USE, THIS TECHNIQUE WILL NOT WORK!!! Once you have the word, then you need to feed it back to them, but if you do it too quickly, you might come off as pompous or arrogant.

Feed their answers back to them, but act as if the two of you are discovering something together. Here is an example of how the above hypothetical situation might have continued...

"Okay, let me make sure I'm hearing you correctly. What I'm hearing is that you woke up on Thursday, and you really wanted some time off, is that right? And at some level, you were hoping that the time off might make you feel more confident, I think that's the word you said, is that right? Okay, so let me get this straight, you wanted to feel more confident, and one of the ways in the past that you've accomplished that was by playing hooky, right? Okay, so then I guess what I'm hearing here is that what you really wanted was to feel confident, but you didn't know any other way to achieve that Thursday morning than by way of calling in sick. Is that accurate? Then what I'm hearing is you really wanted to feel confident, and if you had gotten that some other way, you wouldn't have needed to take the time off, because what you really wanted was to feel that confident feeling, not to take time off, right?"

Now by doing it in this sort of self-discovering way, it gives the impression that you both are figuring this out together. It is possible, although unlikely, that your client may disagree with you at the end, and if this happens, just get to a higher level of emotional benefit. Simply say, "Oh, I'm sorry, then if you had the time off, and felt confident, what would that have done for you emotionally?" Now start back at the top, run through the process again until you get agreement.

Once you have the emotional need, help the client link that emotion up to a new behavior. Link it up to a positive activity. And the more you can link that activity to achieving their outcomes, the better the result will be.

Notes

This is extremely powerful when using hypnosis and NLP, because the link can happen at the conscious <u>and</u> unconscious levels immediately. You can learn more about how to use these techniques at our NLP Practitioner Training.

Notes

Self-Coaching

While it's not always optimal, it is definitely possible to coach yourself. The tools and techniques in this book can all be used by you, for you and with yourself.

Self-coaching is possible and can be effective. Remember, though, that we are all thinking inside our own box. It is often difficult to see options and opportunities outside of our own box. Because perception is projection, we can tend to see our problem everywhere we look.

A useful technique for this is Perceptual Positions. Sometimes we are able to get out of our own boxes just by assuming the different Perceptual Positions. The more you do this, the better you'll get.

When you're ready for a very powerful and effective one-on-one coaching relationship, give us a call. Our methods go way beyond the basics you're learning here, and our results are guaranteed. Call Transform Destiny at 800-497-6614 or 714-408-4281 to enroll in our **Inner Circle** programs.

We normally live our lives with our attention scattered like the light coming out of a light bulb. When you're aligned with an incredible coach, your focus will be laser intense and your outcomes will be achieved.

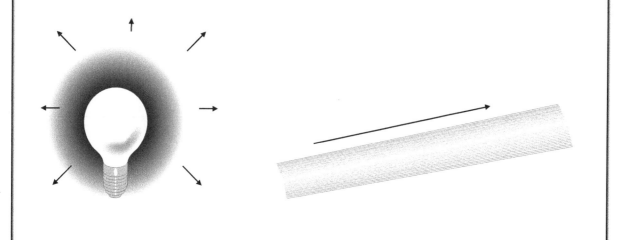

Notes

Sample Forms

Notes

Sample Application Form

Please fill out this application in its entirety

☐ **YES, Michael!** I want to surround myself with positive, motivated people and get coached to success! I understand that not everyone is accepted into the program and that applying does not imply I will be accepted.

Full Name: _____

Email: _____

Address 1: _____

Address 2: _____

City, St, Zip: _____

Phone: _____ **Mobile:** _____

What are the three goals you want to accomplish in the next 12 months?

1. _____

2. _____

3. _____

What are the biggest challenges you are facing right now?

_____

_____

_____

_____

_____

_____

Notes

Name the key people in your life and what they provide for you:

_____

_____

_____

_____

Rate your business experience (Circle one):

None   A Little   Average   Experienced   Expert

How many hours per week do you work: _____

How many hours per week do you WANT to work: _____

How many businesses do you own/control: _____

What is your current gross income? $ _____

What is your desired income goal in 12 months? $ _____

What would you say have been your greatest accomplishments to date:

_____

_____

_____

_____

_____

_____

I'm willing to give/receive help for the mutual benefit of the Mastermind group (Circle one):

No   It Depends   Maybe   Probably   Absolutely

Notes

I'm willing to invest in tools, systems and education to accomplish my goals (Circle one):

No   It Depends   Maybe   Probably   Absolutely

Coaching and Masterminds of successful peers are essential to my success (Circle one):

No   It Depends   Maybe   Probably   Absolutely

What is the most attractive aspect to you about the Inner Circle Coaching Program: _____

_____

_____

Have you ever been in a coaching/mastermind program before: Yes   No

If so, with whom: _____

Briefly describe why you're a good candidate for this program (use back, if necessary): ____

_____

_____

_____

_____

Notes

Sample Success Coaching Agreement

Client Name: _____

This agreement, between Transform Destiny, Inc. and the above named client will begin on _____ and will continue for a minimum of _____ months. Based on this commitment, the fee per month will be $_____, pre-paid, or $_____ per month, due in advance, each month.

The services to be provided by the coach to the client are coaching and tele-coaching, as designed jointly with the client. Coaching, which is not advice, therapy or counseling, may address specific personal projects, business successes, or general conditions in the client's life or profession. Other coaching services include values clarification, brainstorming, identifying plans of action, and examining models of operating in life, asking clarifying questions, and making empowering requests.

Upon completion of the duration of this coaching relationship, coaching will convert to a month-to-month basis, unless other arrangements are made prior to that date. The client and coach agree to provide one another with a fourteen day notice in the event a cancellation is requested. Cancellation fees apply, and will include fees covering the remainder of the coaching sessions agreed to, or one month of coaching fees, whichever is the smaller. It should be noted that an average of four weeks per month is used in calculating the monthly fee. Transform Destiny, Inc. promises the client that all information provided to the corporation and to the coach will be kept strictly confidential.

Throughout the working relationship, the coach will engage in direct and personal conversations. The client can count on the coach to be honest and straightforward in asking questions and making requests. The client understands that the power of the coaching relationship can only be granted by the client, and the client agrees to do just that — have the coaching relationship be powerful. If the client believes the coaching is not working as desired, the client will communicate and take action to return the power to the coaching relationship.

Our signatures on this agreement indicate full understanding of the agreement with the information outlined above.

_____   _____

Client   Date   Coach   Date

Notes

Sample Success Coaching Action Plan

Use this form to write down specific to-dos and long-term goals

To Dos

Action Item   **Due Date**

☐ _____   _____

☐ _____   _____

☐ _____   _____

☐ _____   _____

☐ _____   _____

☐ _____   _____

☐ _____   _____

☐ _____   _____

☐ _____   _____

☐ _____   _____

Short-Term Goals   *Long-Term Outcomes*

_____   _____

_____   _____

_____   _____

_____   _____

_____   _____

_____   _____

_____   _____

_____   _____
I agree to complete these action items by the date due (Sign)   Date

Notes

Marketing Bonus

The following are some ideas to help you get started, and market yourself in an economic way. Please keep in mind, there are exceptions to every rule, and depending upon your demographic location, these tips will have greater effect in some places than in others.

1. Join your Chamber of Commerce:

When someone joins the Chamber of Commerce, it says, "I am employed, and I have disposable income, and I'm willing to invest it in things that will help me succeed." In addition to marketing yourself to gainfully employed people who will be able to hire you for hypnotherapy services, most members of Chambers of Commerce support heavily the idea of referrals and networking. Unfortunately, most people join Chambers thinking that once they join, the business will start to roll in. This is not true. You must take time to cultivate relationships inside the chamber. If you are a consistent presence in your chamber, it will eventually pay off.

2. Use Vista Print for marketing needs:

In the beginning of your business, there is no need to hire a printing company to customize brochures and business cards. Start with the generic brochures, business cards, letterhead, and envelopes designed by Vista Print. You can reach them at www.VistaPrint.com. Once you are producing a consistent income, then you may want to upgrade to a more professional media print or qualify for bulk rates. For now, Vista Print will work just fine.

3. Speak whenever you can, wherever you can:

Health clubs, yoga studios, hair salons, martial arts studios, book stores, Chambers of Commerce, schools, spiritual centers and churches – all of these places are usually very willing to have guest speakers. Create a 30-minute presentation that you can use to enlighten people on the benefits of hypnosis. When you are finished with your presentation, leave plenty of your brochures and business cards so they can contact you if they are interested.

4. Use executive office suites for office space:

Most people believe that the first thing they need to do is rent a beautiful office in order to start their business. THIS IS THE LAST THING YOU SHOULD DO. First, start off with

Notes

executive office suites. These are offices that you can rent by the hour. They are fully furnished, and all you have to do is bring in your stereo and framed certification to place on the bookshelf, and you have a mobile office. No, they probably won't have recliners for your client to sit in, but they will have comfortable chairs that will work quite well. Once you are working enough to spend more money on executive office suites, then you know it is time to rent an office of your own. Another viable option is for you to find 5 locations strategically located within a specific geographic area and work one day each week out of each office. You can maximize your advertising dollar this way.

5. Set up a merchant account:

The public will perceive your company as being much more stable if you can accept Visa and MasterCard. Remember, everyone may not have $300 cash, but almost everyone has $300 on a credit card. You are much more apt to receive business if you can accept credit cards. PayPal, Square and Stripe have professional merchant services.

6. Get a toll-free number:

Even if you are only doing business locally, a toll-free number will convince your clients that you are serious about your business and can make you look more successful than even your largest competitor. Contrary to popular belief, toll-free numbers are not expensive if you go with the right provider. Try www.FreedomVoice.com. They have rates as low as $10 /mo for an introductory toll-free system with five voicemail boxes and the ability to forward calls to any phone on a time scale (so curious people don't wake you up at 3am!)

7. Write a book.

Nothing makes you more of an authority than writing a book. It's easier than you may think. I wrote my best-selling book, *Learn Hypnosis... Now!*, after attending this very course years ago. While the task may seem daunting, once you know the step-by-step formula, you can have your book done in no time. Visit www.YouCanBecomeAnAuthor.com to learn about our book writing/publishing course.

Notes

8. Send emails and postcards to past clientele five times each year.

Believe it or not, your clients will forget your name and lose your phone number. But if you remain in contact with them throughout the year, they will be able to send you referrals when people ask how they lost weight or stopped smoking.

Send both business correspondence as well as personal emails to keep your business top of mind. The service at www.SendOutCards.com is a great way to keep in touch automatically.

9. Don't Sell Coaching Sessions:

One of the biggest reasons why most coaches are "flat broke" is because they try to sell packages of coaching sessions. For example, one session, six sessions, twelve sessions, etc.

Successful coaches create coaching programs: multi-tiered programs where each successive level gets more access to the coach and, thereby, easier and faster results.

For example:

- Group coaching program: no one-on-one time with the coach
- Silver: group coaching and masterminds – only group time with the coach
- Gold: Silver plus coaching calls – individual attention from the coach
- Platinum: Gold plus more calls and VIP day (NLP)
- Diamond: Platinum plus "done for you" components

10. Join a Successful Coaching Program

Nothing is better for accelerating your results than learning from the "inside" by experience and being mentored by someone who has had success in the area you are wanting to be successful.

Our Inner Circle program will give you direct access to Transform Destiny founder and successful coach, Michael Stevenson.

Talk to your trainer about the possibility of joining our Inner Circle.

Notes

Ad Success Sheet

Place Ad Copy Here

Name of Paper:

Investment:

Circulation of Paper:

Days Run: Sun   Mon   Tue   Wed   Thu   Fri   Sat

Number of Weeks:

Section(s) Used:

Contact Person:

Comments:

Number of Calls Received:

Number of Appointments Scheduled:

_____ ÷ _____ = _____
Investment   Appointments   Cost Per Appt

Note: If run for multiple weeks, formula for Cost Per Appt. will need to be modified.

Notes

Helpful Hints for Dynamic Brochures

A personal brochure is a prospecting tool designed to attract new clients to your practice. Its purpose is to establish a positive emotional bond between you and the reader before you ever meet. A well-designed and carefully written personal brochure conveys credibility and competence while at the same time making the reader feel comfortable in picking up the phone to call you. Unless it achieves those results, your brochure will be worthless, no matter how it looks or what it contains.

The personal brochure is your first opportunity to establish a strong foundation for future business relationships. It is *not* the place to impress potential clients with your products or to score resume points. Take full advantage of this opportunity, and make your personal brochure work hard for you.

Notes

© 2018 Transform Destiny • www.transformdestiny.com • 800-497-6614

Five Steps to Creating an Effective Personal Brochure

Step One: Pick a Single, Focused Benefit

You cannot be all things to all people. Select a specific benefit that is designed to attract your target market. The most effective personal brochures tell a story or give examples which showcase this benefit in an interesting way. Keep these questions in mind: "What single benefit is most important to my potential clients, and what can I share about myself which will drive this point home?"

Step Two: Write a Personal Biography

Regardless of what you are selling – financial services, widgets, consulting, or coaching – if you don't do a good job selling yourself, your products will remain on the shelf. By the time a potential client finishes reading your personal brochure, he or she should feel as if they really know you. Present the information as though you are sharing a part of yourself. Like a good Barbara Walters interview, you can establish this kind of rapport by revealing who you are as a human being, not as a salesperson. Include personal information which illustrates who you are and builds an emotional connection between you and the reader.

Your personal biography should account from half to three-quarters of the brochure's entire contents. Resist the temptation to talk about your therapeutic services for at least the first two paragraphs. Even though you are selling yourself, don't frame it as a hard sales pitch. If the reader feels that you are pushing yourself on them, they will be less likely to do business with you.

If your practice is affiliated with a company, limit company and service information to one or two paragraphs. Present your company as a support system and capitalize on the power of your company name. The link between your image and your established company name increases your credibility in the minds of potential consumers.

Step Three: Follow These General Writing Guidelines

Use the third person, objective point of view in writing the text. Third person gives the impression that you are reporting facts, not engaging in self-important bragging. Keep the text positive.

Notes

Present your material in paragraphs. As much as salespeople don't believe it, long story-formatted text outsells short text every time. Use bullets sparingly as they can break up the natural flow of an idea.

Step Four: Create a Knockout Cover and an Appealing Layout

The central design element of your personal brochure is the front cover. The most compelling personal biography, or the most creative and effective presentation of your business philosophy is meaningless unless your prospects actually pick up the brochure in the first place. The cover must stimulate a reader's curiosity, announcing loudly and unmistakably, "Pick Me Up!" Do not place any images or text on the cover that refer directly to your company, products or services. Large format covers attract more attention, so use a large formatted image that is easily recognized by your target market.

Your personal brochure should be inviting to the eye, making the reader want to start and finish it. Include lots of open (or white) space. Don't clutter the design by cramming it with long, dense blocks of text or too many photographs or graphics. In addition to a generous use of white space, photographs and graphics will give your brochure a look of professionalism. As important as the content is, the look and feel of your brochure convey more about your image than words ever will. A well-designed brochure builds instant credibility in the reader's mind.

Unusual sized brochures dramatically increase readership rates. The best shape for brochures is usually a square, because it is often perceived as an invitation. The most effective brochure sizes, when folded, are 6"x 6", 7"x 7", or 8"x 8".

Step Five: Purchase High-Quality Typesetting & Printing

In today's highly competitive, technologically savvy business world, using full- or four-color to print your marketing materials is an absolute must. Full-color design dramatically increases readability as well as overall impact. While customized brochures are ideally the way to go, a close second would be using stock papers such as Paper Direct. This option should be used only if you cannot afford professional customized printing.

Use serif fonts, 9 to 12 points in size and set left justified to make your brochure easy to read. Print your brochure on good quality, heavy paper --100 lb. gloss cover stock is best. Prospective clients' perceptions of you are strongly influenced by the physical feel of your brochure more

Notes

than what they read inside. We recommend that you use a commercial printer that prints a 175-line screen or higher on a four-color press.

Personal Brochure Uses

The purpose of your personal brochure is to attract new clients. Be lavish in distributing them. Don't hoard them. They can't do the job they were designed to do if they sit in a box under your desk or on shelves in the back room. We have found that the clients who get the best results from their personal brochures are those who print in quantities of at least 2500 and usually 5,000 or 10,000. With a generous print run, you won't worry about running out and you will feel comfortable and eager to distribute them.

So, where should you use your personal brochure? In any and every situation where you would normally use your business card.

Networking

Telemarketing

Lead Follow-up

Potential Clients

Advertising

Presentations

Current Clients

Public Speaking

Guidelines for Writing Your Personal Biography

People do business with people they feel comfortable with. Sharing your personal story gives you a chance to introduce prospective clients, not to an intimidating coach, but to a real, caring person, someone with similar concerns and interests, someone who makes them feel, "S/he's just like me!"

One approach you can use to develop your personal story is the "self-interview." You can conduct this interview yourself, or ask a friend or family member to do it. Record the information either into a tape recorder or by writing it down. Record your answers and use them as the basis when your write your personal brochure.

1. What has been your greatest accomplishment in life so far?

Notes

2. Describe the most difficult challenge you have ever faced. How did you meet it? What did you learn from it?

3. Describe an important lesson you learned from someone in your family. Who taught you the lesson? How has that lesson influenced you?

4. What single life-experience has created the person you are today?

5. If you had to limit your life to one point in time, what would you say was the defining moment? What about this moment made it so significant?

Notes

© 2018 Transform Destiny • www.transformdestiny.com • 800-497-6614

Additional Reference Materials

Notes

The Psychology of Suggestions

What is a suggestion?

1. A suggestion is any single thought, series of thoughts, ideas, words, beliefs, or actions given in any manner – direct, indirect, conscious, unconscious, that changes or alters a person's normal behavior pattern.

2. A suggestion is any process whereby a person accepts a command, a plea, a proposition, a thought, idea, belief, or any direction to be acted upon in the absence of any critical or reflective thoughts which would normally occur.

3. A suggestion is any process whereby one person or group may have subtle or direct influence on another's behavior in any state whether it be the conscious, unconscious, or hypnotic state.

Suggestions come in a variety of ways. They influence us every day of our lives and have done so since the day of our birth. Below are a few examples of the types of suggestions that may have had a bearing on changing or altering our normal behavior patterns.

Direct Suggestions are any verbal statement or physical action that is direct, to the point and without camouflage. Direct suggestions are given in an "authoritarian" or "persuasive" manner.

- Everybody stand up. (authoritarian)

- Everybody stand up, please. (persuasive)

- Pass the sugar.

- Come here.

- Eat your food.

Indirect/Inferred Suggestions are generally not recognized as suggestions. This is because they are primarily non-verbal, often only motions or sounds, and the subject is not even aware of their influence.

Notes

Indirect:

- Cough ... and you cause others to cough.

- Yawn ... and you cause others to yawn.

- Smile ... and you cause others to smile.

- Look up at tall buildings... and you cause others to look up.

Inferred:

- Pointing a finger at someone, suggesting they come here

- Pointing a finger at someone, suggesting they leave the room

- Nodding your head to indicate your approval or disapproval

- Making a fist at someone, suggesting violent action

Prestige Suggestions are those you accept and act upon as your very own without "second thought" or contradiction because they were given by a person of prestige whom you like, trust, respect or in whom have some confidence. Prestige suggestions may enhance your life in some way – socially, economically, politically, academically, emotionally, intellectually, physically or psychologically.

Examples of people who have prestige:

- Doctor
- Lawyer
- Teacher
- Clergy
- Politician
- Coaches

- Speakers
- Friends
- Parents
- Authors
- Entertainers
- Athletes

Notes

© 2018 Transform Destiny • www.transformdestiny.com • 800-497-6614

Non-Prestige Suggestions are personalized conditioned reflex suggestions that influence a person's conduct in the waking state.

- Music suggests happiness, sadness, dancing, singing, romance, etc.

- Sight or smell of food suggests hunger, or possibly nausea.

- Rain suggests freshness, cleanliness, depression, coziness, etc.

- Street noises suggest hyperactivity or excitement.

Environmental Suggestions are those that affect your 5 human senses, VAKOG (Visual, Auditory, Kinesthetic, Olfactory, Gustatory)

- Clear sunny days with bright blue skies and comfortable temperatures make us feel happy, content and full of vitality.

- Dismal gray days of rain, snow, or fog make us feel "down in the dumps" or sluggish.

- Extreme heat or cold can generate feelings of discomfort or pain.

- Well-decorated or well-ventilated working or living conditions can cause us to react with a feeling of well-being and elation.

Conditioned Reflex Suggestions cause a person to form a habit pattern or way of life based on a continuous, constant, repetitive learning process. This learning process is reflex conditioning, and it can be a conscious or a subconscious process that will influence or alter a person's behavior pattern with or without his/her awareness. Conditioned reflex suggestions affect all five of the human senses and they can be self-induced or externally induced.

- Good Humor man rings his bells, you automatically buy his ice cream

- Parades, mob violence, political rallies, all may stimulate your physical/emotional responses

- Religious ceremonies accept dogmas and doctrines without question

- Vulgarity or obscenities stimulate positive or negative emotions or physical responses

Notes

Emotional Suggestions are those that raise your emotional or sensory state thereby setting into motion any feelings, sensations or emotional responses.

- Shouting/making verbal threats can cause a state of fear or panic

- Antagonizing can cause anger

- Gentleness/empathy can cause happiness, laughter or crying

Unconscious Suggestions are those comments, statements, suggestions or stimuli received by a person while in some form of altered, receptive state which an outside source absent-mindedly or indiscreetly induces. Generally, neither part is consciously aware of the consequences.

Social Suggestions are those suggestions designed to lead or appeal to an individual for the purpose of conformity. Experiments in social suggestions show that people tend to "follow the crowd." Individuals "give in" to peer pressure.

- Politics – people tend to vote for the person who appears to be "the peoples' choice"

- In the world of fashion – people "follow the trends." To be in style is to be accepted. It is a way of belonging and being "in" with the crowd by inference.

Autosuggestion is the process of giving suggestions to one's self, either in the "waking state" or any "alpha or meditative state".

Hetero-Suggestions are those given by one person to another in any manner.

Negative Suggestions are designed to tell the client not to manifest something, be it a behavior, emotion or thought.

- Don't feel stressed.

- Don't get angry.

- You will not smoke.

- Don't roll your eyes at me.

While generally not recommended to use in hypnosis, negative suggestions can sometimes produce a desirable effect:

- Don't agree too quickly.

- Don't smile as you think about your future.

- Don't enjoy this process too much.

Notes

Words that may indicate negative suggestions are being used:

Try	Maybe	Hope
Never	Don't	Can't

Positive Suggestions are designed to create images of the desired outcome.

- Do feel happy.
- You can relax deeply.
- You will succeed.

Words that may indicate positive suggestions are being used:

Succeed	Will	Know
Always	Do	Can

Notes

Glossary

ABREACTION - The release of emotionally charged material from the mental process.

ANXIETY- Painful uneasiness of mind.

AUTO-CONDITIONING - A series of experiments designed for bringing one's subconscious under control.

CONDITIONED REFLEX - A reflex that responds automatically.

CONDITIONING - A series of inductions making certain ideas or things acceptable to the subject's subconscious mind.

CONSCIOUS - State of being aware of an inward state or an outside fact.

CONSCIOUS DISTORTION - Responses to the senses lessened in degree by interference during consciousness.

DISSOCIATION - The segregation from consciousness of certain components of mental processes, which then function independently.

DIANETICS - Science founded by mathematician Hubbard, utilizing, but not admitting to, all the principles of hypnotism.

EMOTIONAL OUTLET- A habit pattern formed to release emotional tension.

NLP- Neuro-Linguistic Programming; The study of success, communication and excellence.

OBJECTIVITY- Ability to view events, ideas and phenomena as external and apart from self-consciousness, detached and impersonal.

PHOBIA- Morbid fear.

PROJECTION - The attributing of one's own feelings to someone else.

RAPPORT- Relation of harmony, comfort, accord; state of being in tune with your subject.

SELF RAPPORT- Being in tune with one's self.

SUBCONSCIOUS- The nature of mental operation not yet present in consciousness.

SUBJECT- One who is experimented with or tested.

SUBMODALITIES- The finer distinctions of the pictures, sounds, feelings, smells, tastes and self-talk in our mind.

TIME TECHNIQUES- A set of tools based on NLP that allows you to instantly eliminate bad feelings and thoughts, as well as putting compelling goals into your future so they absolutely happen.

TRAUMA - Injury; shock or the resulting condition.

WILL- A thought conveyed by the subconscious that becomes reality.

WILL, CONSCIOUS- Imaginary mental force.

WORD ASSOCIATION - Mental reaction to word stimuli.

Notes

Training Contacts & Networks

Keep in touch with us and with those who you meet and connect with at the training. Make note of all your contacts' information here:

Name	Phone	Email	Notes
Transform Destiny	800-497-6614	cs@transformdestiny.com	Success experts